The Uncanny

Peter Hepplewhite ⚬ Neil Tonge

Hamlyn Children's

Publisher: Zuza Vrbova
Editor: Richard Widdows
Art Editor: Donna Payne
Designer: Linda Males
Illustrations: Nick Farmer and Andrew Elliot of Storyboards Harpers
Picture Researcher: Suzanne Williams
Production: Christine Campbell
Cover design: Ian Butterworth

Consultant: Philip Mantle of the British UFO Research Association

069393 Picture Credits

Bruce Coleman: page 26 (Stephen J Krasemann), page 27 (Jane Burton);
Colorsport: page 36;
Robert Harding Picture Library: page 19 top (Paul van Riel), page 19 bottom
(FPG International);
Hulton Getty Picture Collection: page 33, page 40;
Images Colour Library: page 8;
Kobal Collection: page 41;
Mary Evans Picture Library: page 11, page 18, page 20;
Peter Newark's Historical & American Pictures: page 9, page 10, page 17;
Photodisc Inc.: cover;
Science Photo Library: page 28 (European Space Agency), page 34
(Philippe Plailly Images).

Published in 1997 by Hamlyn Children's Books, an imprint of Reed International Books,
Michelin House, 81 Fulham Road, London SW3 6RB and Auckland and Melbourne
Illustrations © 1997 Reed International Books Limited
Text © 1997 Peter Hepplewhite & Neil Tonge
The authors have asserted their moral rights.
ISBN 0 600 59296 0
First Edition
10 9 8 7 6 5 4 3 2 1
A CIP catalogue record for this book is available from the British Library.
Printed in Italy by Olivotto

Contents

Introducing more great titles in
The Unexplained series.

When it comes to the world of the supernatural and the paranormal, there's a lot to talk about. Together with *The Uncanny*, these are the other brilliant books in this brand new series hot off the Hamlyn production line.

ALIEN ❯❯ ENCOUNTERS

Close connections of the extra-terrestrial kind

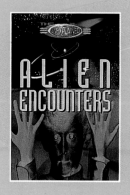

❮❮ MYSTERIOUS PLACES

Strange happenings in remote regions

HAUNTINGS ❯❯

Spooky travels through time and space

The Uncanny

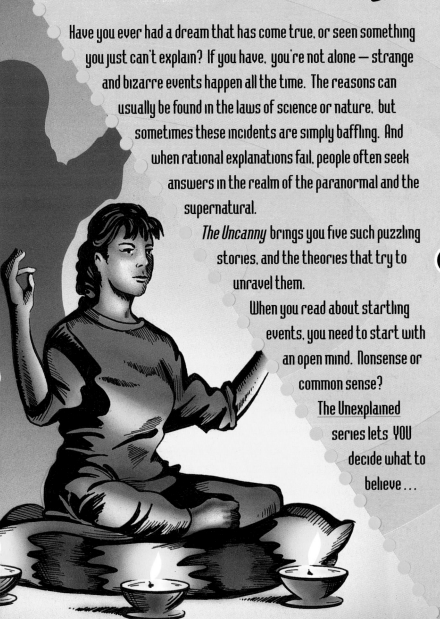

Have you ever had a dream that has come true, or seen something you just can't explain? If you have, you're not alone — strange and bizarre events happen all the time. The reasons can usually be found in the laws of science or nature, but sometimes these incidents are simply baffling. And when rational explanations fail, people often seek answers in the realm of the paranormal and the supernatural.

The Uncanny brings you five such puzzling stories, and the theories that try to unravel them.

When you read about startling events, you need to start with an open mind. Nonsense or common sense?

<u>The Unexplained</u> series lets YOU decide what to believe...

TO KILL A KING

The plot to kill King James VI, Scotland's last monarch, was discovered by accident. David Seaton, the local deputy bailiff, had heard troubling rumours about his maid, Gilly Duncan. It was said that the girl wandered over the countryside at night, and healed sick people with magic powers during the day.

Seaton questioned her and found the "Devil's mark" on her throat. He had no doubts that she was indeed a witch!

Gilly was put in prison and tortured until she gave the names of other "witches". Terrified, hurt and confused, she made up a long list. Among those people she accused were Agnes Simpson, a midwife, and Dr John Cunningham, secretary to the Earl of Bothwell — one of the most powerful nobles in Scotland. Gilly confessed that Cunningham often led them all in wild dances at night ... and wrote down oaths to serve Satan.

DATE:

1590

PLACE:

North Berwick, Scotland

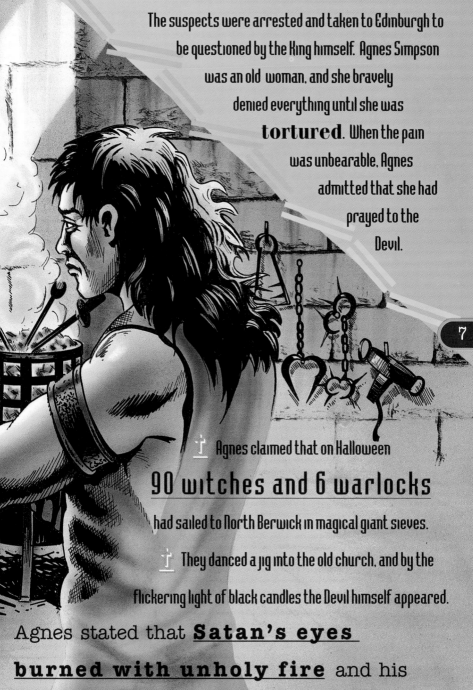

The suspects were arrested and taken to Edinburgh to be questioned by the King himself. Agnes Simpson was an old woman, and she bravely denied everything until she was **tortured**. When the pain was unbearable, Agnes admitted that she had prayed to the Devil.

Agnes claimed that on Halloween

90 witches and 6 warlocks

had sailed to North Berwick in magical giant sieves.

They danced a jig into the old church, and by the flickering light of black candles the Devil himself appeared. Agnes stated that **Satan's eyes burned with unholy fire** and his **feet and hands were hooked claws**.

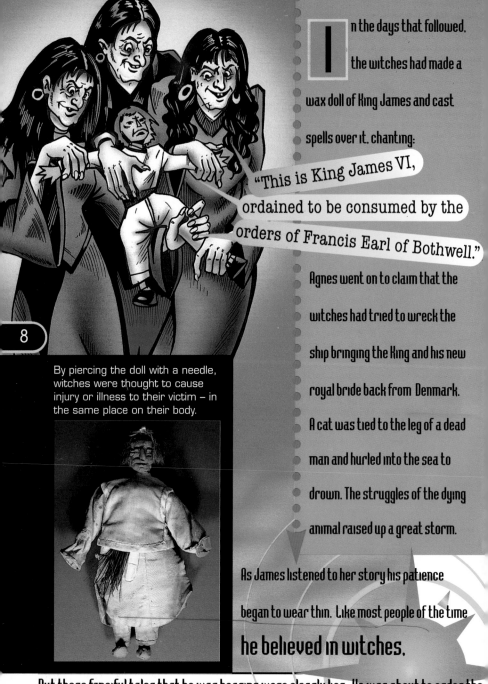

I n the days that followed, the witches had made a wax doll of King James and cast spells over it, chanting:

"This is King James VI, ordained to be consumed by the orders of Francis Earl of Bothwell."

Agnes went on to claim that the witches had tried to wreck the ship bringing the King and his new royal bride back from Denmark. A cat was tied to the leg of a dead man and hurled into the sea to drown. The struggles of the dying animal raised up a great storm.

By piercing the doll with a needle, witches were thought to cause injury or illness to their victim – in the same place on their body.

As James listened to her story his patience began to wear thin. Like most people of the time **he believed in witches,** But these fanciful tales that he was hearing were clearly lies. He was about to order the release of all these strange prisoners when a really unexpected thing happened ...

Agnes was upset that the King didn't believe her. She called him over and spoke to him quietly.

And she repeated, word for word, the private talk of James and his bride on their wedding night.

The King was astonished. How could she know such things? He had been <u>alone</u> with his new Queen. This was clearly powerful magic and he ordered the "witches" to be put on trial. Gilly, Agnes, Cunningham and many others were found guilty of **WITCHCRAFT**.

witchcraft

They were **burned** at the stake

on Castle Hill, Edinburgh in 1591. The Earl of Bothwell was also arrested, but he escaped and fled abroad.

Theory 1 ⇨ A Murderous Plot

Some experts believe that Bothwell did run a coven of witches at North Berwick, and tried to use evil magic to murder the King.

Francis, the Earl of Bothwell, was a cousin of James VI — and he had a claim to the throne of Scotland. He may have appeared to his followers disguised as the Devil, and used Cunningham to organise them. And Agnes Simpson could have repeated the King's words to his bride, because she had been told them by Bothwell, who had a spy in the royal court. Magic wouldn't really have killed James VI, but the coven believed it could — and so did the King.

A "witch-hunt" led by Puritans at Salem in colonial America led to the death of 19 women in 1692.

Three women being executed in Germany in 1555. "Witches" were burnt to "cleanse their evil spirits".

Theory 2 ⇨ Fear, Torture and Death

During these times there were "witch panics" all over Europe and in the American colonies. Many totally innocent victims suffered from persecution, and a suspected witch faced terrible tortures. In Scotland a Spanish instrument known as the **strappado** was used. The woman's arms were tied behind her back, and she was hoisted off the ground; then heavy weights were fastened to her feet until her shoulders tore from their sockets.

After treatment like this, most people would say anything to stop the pain. But when they "confessed" they were killed for being witches …

The North Berwick witches told such fantastic tales that James VI almost allowed them to go free. To this day, nobody knows what Agnes said to the King that fateful night — or why she tried to convince him that she was guilty.

Perhaps she was so frightened that she had come to believe her own stories.

The Power of Magic

Throughout history deaths, diseases, floods and famines have all shown how little control people have over the power of nature.

In 16th-century Europe, belief in supernatural forces was a way of coming to terms with bad luck in life.

Unable to explain events with science, most ordinary people relied on magic.

They thought that ghosts, goblins, spirits, charms, potions and wise men or women had the power to cause or change all sorts of natural events. Magic could be used to save a sick child, win over a lover, or curse a neighbour.

12

The Christian Church taught that all magic was evil and that people should not try to change God's will. Witches were blamed for many of the troubles in the world. In March 1550 the Bishop of Salisbury wrote this warning to Queen Elizabeth I of England:

"Witches and sorcerers are marvellously increased within Your Grace's realm. Your Grace's subjects pine away unto death, their colour fadeth, their flesh rotteth, their speech is benumbed. The shoal of such malefactors [criminals] is great, their doings horrible."

Witchcraft became a crime punishable by death. Between 1542 and 1682 over **1,000 witches** were executed in England. Often they were helpless women, accused by nasty neighbours of causing misfortunes, such as the death of a child or failure of their crops.

13

How to defeat a witch's curse

This is a counter-spell from 17th-century Scotland:

"The eye that goes over me and through me, the eye that pierces to the bone and the marrow, I will overthrow and the elements will help me."

THE MAD MONK

Alexei, the young son of the Tsar, and heir to the Russian throne, lay on his bed in great pain. He had fallen while playing and begun bleeding internally, causing his joints to swell up. Alexei had inherited haemophilia from his mother, and the slightest fall triggered unstoppable bleeding.

The doctors shook their heads in despair, and all his parents could do was pray.

But Nicholas and Alexandra had other ideas. Two years previously, stories had reached the Tsar and Tsarina of a holy man whose cures of illnesses seemed to defy the skill and knowledge of the doctors. The holder of these uncanny powers was Grigori Rasputin. Towards midnight, on the day of Alexei's fall, Rasputin was smuggled into the royal palace.

DATE:

July 1907

PLACE:

Tsarkoye Palace, St Petersburg, Russia

He made a strange sight among the splendour of the palace, with his dark, greasy hair and matted, tangled beard.

Falling to his knees, Rasputin began to pray over the small boy and then gently talk to him, all the while **STARING AT HIM WITH HIS PIERCING EYES**. For a while he held his hand over the swelling joints, telling the boy that the bleeding would cease and the joints would return to normal.

> "Believe in the power of my prayer and your son will live."

Rasputin said to the anxious parents, as he calmed them down. *Then, as if by a miracle, they saw their son smile and drop into a deep, restful sleep.*

What Happened to Rasputin?

A fter the holy man's miraculous cure of their son, the Tsar and Tsarina came to trust him completely. This worried the palace courtiers and they became jealous of Rasputin's influence. Once, they did manage to have this powerful figure banned from court, but he was soon back in favour.

The outbreak of **World War 1** in **1914**

marked the beginning of the end for both Rasputin and the Russian royal family. Rasputin had warned the Tsar not to fight Germany and her allies, but his advice was quickly forgotten. The war soon started to go badly for Russia and the people needed a "scapegoat" to blame. Rasputin, not the Tsar, was the unfortunate victim.

The knives were out for "the mad monk".

In December 1916 Rasputin was invited to a

late-night party by a group of Russian aristocrats.

He was offered poisoned cakes and wine — and he took both.

Yet despite having enough to kill several people, he was not affected.

In sheer desperation, (Prince Yusopov,) the leader of the conspiracy, then shot him in the back.

Rasputin was pronounced D E A D and the

relieved plotters began to celebrate.

>>>>> Suddenly the holy man jumped to his feet and fled from the building.

He was pursued into the night and finally caught by the conspirators.

In panic they shot him several more times – before dumping his body through a hole in the nearby frozen river.

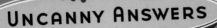

Theory 1 ⇨ Hypnotic Powers

Everybody who met Rasputin recalled his piercing blue eyes and his hypnotic voice.

18

It has been suggested that he was able to give temporary relief to his patients by putting them in a sort of controlled trance. In this hypnotic state people can blot out everyday sights, sounds, memories and information to focus on one particular object or idea. This might not cure them, but it could certainly help the patient to control their suffering — even a young boy.

Death of the Russian Royal Family

Shortly before his murder, Rasputin had written to the Tsarina, predicting that the royal family would not survive his own death.

The following year a Communist revolution overtook Russia — and the royal family were executed by a firing squad.

At the time that Rasputin was alive, Russia was a deeply religious country.

The Eastern Orthodox Church had both power and money. Many peasants thought that the Tsar and his family were specially chosen by God, and almost holy themselves. Mere pictures of saints were believed to be powerful enough to bring about cures for disease and illness.

There were many hundreds of holy men wandering about Russia at that time, all of them claiming that they had special powers. There were many people, and not just the superstitious peasants, who believed it was possible for these men to work medical miracles.

19

The Royal Touch

from the Middle Ages into the 19th century, both English and French kings were thought to have special gifts of healing.

Edward the Confessor, King of England until 1066, was one monarch thought to have healing power. His holy quality is conveyed by the halo round his royal head.

One particular disease they claimed to cure was known as **"scrofula"** or the **"king's evil"**, where the victim's face broke out in unpleasant sores and growths.

There are many people who believe it is possible for their religious faith to cure illness. One of the most famous holy places for such pilgrimages is **Lourdes,** a small town with a Roman Catholic shrine in south-west France.

Faith Healing

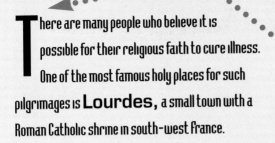

It was here that a young peasant girl named Bernadette claimed to have seen religious visions in 1858.

21

The site soon attracted thousands, and still does today. Despite this, only 64 cases have been declared "miracles" by the Church.

An extraordinary cure was experienced by one young Italian pilgrim. He travelled to Lourdes more than a year after being told that he had cancer in his bones. **The disease had eaten away so badly at his left leg that it had become detached from the hip bone.**

Scarcely had he arrived in Lourdes when he found his appetite returning and the pain easing. Returning to his doctor, he was X-rayed — and it was indeed discovered that the cancer was fast disappearing.

HECTOR THE HOMING DOG

Hector was lost on Vancouver docks. His master was first Officer on the Dutch cargo ship, the *Simaloer*. But in the frantic rush to load fuel, supplies and cargo, Hector had been left behind when the *Simaloer* sailed for Yokohama, in Japan.

DATE: April 1922

PLACE: Vancouver, Canada

The officer had thought that his pet was safe on board, but Hector had escaped his watchful eye to explore the busy dockside.

Hector's master was upset, but there was nothing he could do about it. Time was money, and ships worked to tight schedules. The Captain wouldn't turn around to collect a missing sailor, let alone a dog.

Hector stood mournfully by the empty space on the quayside, watching the *Simaloer* moving out into the Pacific Ocean.

He whined pitifully and paced up and down, sniffing and looking across the harbour. After a time he knew his owner wouldn't be coming back. Then his instincts took over.

If his master wasn't coming back for him, then he would have to go to his master...

As Hector carefully searched the docks, his unusual behaviour caught the eye of Mr Kiddall. An officer aboard the *SS Hanley*, another steamer preparing for the voyage to Japan, Kiddall watched in fascination as Hector investigated different ships around the busy harbour.

As if he had some plan in mind, the dog boarded, toured and left at least four other vessels.

After a time Kiddall had to go about his duties and he forgot about Hector — but it was not his last sight of the strange dog.

That evening the *SS Hanley* sailed out of Vancouver — with an unusual stowaway on board. When morning came Hector showed himself and settled comfortably in the captain's cabin. The good-natured crew made a fuss of the dog, and looked after him well. Hector accepted their attentions gratefully, but he would not make friends. He remained distant, as if his mind was on other things.

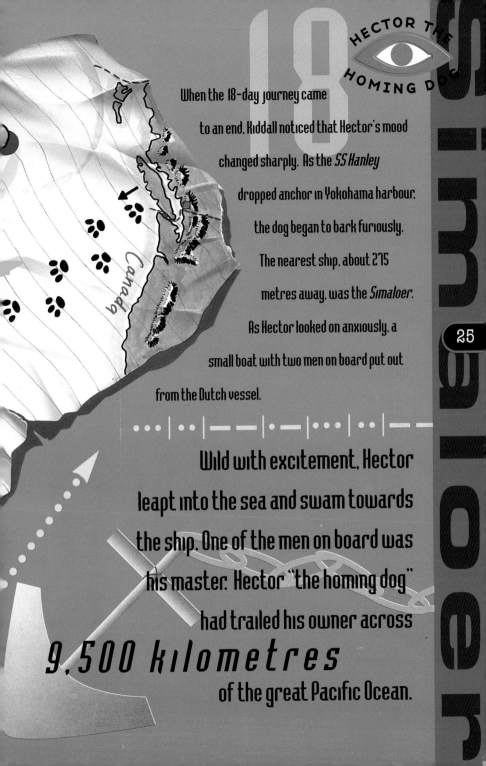

When the 18-day journey came to an end, Kiddall noticed that Hector's mood changed sharply. As the *SS Hanley* dropped anchor in Yokohama harbour, the dog began to bark furiously. The nearest ship, about 275 metres away, was the *Simaloer*. As Hector looked on anxiously, a small boat with two men on board put out from the Dutch vessel.

Canada

Wild with excitement, Hector leapt into the sea and swam towards the ship. One of the men on board was his master. Hector "the homing dog" had trailed his owner across

9,500 kilometres

of the great Pacific Ocean.

How could Hector have known where his master had gone, let alone which ship was heading from Vancouver to Yokohama?

Theory 1 ⇨ Supersenses

Scientists increasingly believe that many creatures have senses that are greater than those of humans.

Over the past **100 years** there have been amazing discoveries about the natural abilities of animals.

Bats can find their way in the dark using an echo location system, or sonar.

Rattlesnakes have heat detectors (just behind their nostrils), which are so sensitive they can detect an approaching animal from temperature changes in the atmosphere.

Migrating birds are among the most remarkable creatures, using natural navigational equipment as sophisticated as any modern plane.

In order to fly "on track" they rely on data from:

- the movement of the Sun during the day, even when it is hidden by thick clouds
- the position of the stars at night
- the strength of the Earth's magnetic field
- checking landmarks en route and recognising the same "home area" every year
- identifying familiar smells

27

It seems likely that mammals such as dogs and cats might have similar abilities.

>>>> for example, a dog's sense of smell is hundreds of times better than a person's.

While the **"supersenses theory"** may explain how a lost dog could find its way home, it does not fully explain Hector's case. His master was on the move – and he had to "track" him across the world's biggest ocean.

The outer core of the centre of the Earth is a mass of swirling molten iron, making the planet like a gigantic magnet. The magnetic field that it generates is weak, but it affects all living things.

In **1996** German scientists conducted an experiment to show how important this field is to birds. They raised garden warbler chicks inside giant magnetic coils that shut them off from the Earth's natural magnetic field. **When the chicks were released in September, their usual migration time, they flew south instead of south-west, 45° in the wrong direction.**

28

It is possible that every individual organism — plants, insects, fish, animals and human beings — have their own unique magnetic "fingerprint". These are linked to the Earth's giant magnetic field and allow sensitive beings to locate others. Perhaps Hector was tracking his master's magnetic print, as if he had a worldwide radar scanner.

If we believe that people have supernatural powers, then why can't animals? Pets and their owners often form special bonds, and some experts suggest that these bonds set up a telepathic link. There are many stories of animals trailing their owners, or warning of disasters before they happen.

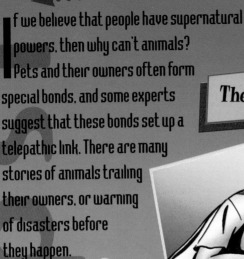

One of the most impressive stories of **"pet tracking"** happened in **1952.**

Head teacher Stacy Woods and his family moved from Anderson, California to a farm near Gage, Oklahoma. Their pet cat, Sugar, was handed over to neighbours because he was terrified of riding in cars.

It was <u>14 months</u> later, as Mrs Woods was milking the cows in the barn, when a cat jumped onto her shoulder: **it was Sugar!**

Owners always just somehow know their pets — but just to make sure she checked the badly shaped bone in his hip. It was him all right. Later on, the Woods family found out that Sugar had vanished three weeks after they had left California. He had spent over a year tracking them down across 2,400 kilometres of rugged country. A strong cat is a good hunter and, despite his poor hip, Sugar had survived by catching prey to eat.

RING OF DEATH

"Sugar" Ray Robinson should have felt confident about his big fight, but he didn't. He was greatly admired for his speed, and ability to box with both hands. Flashing feet and fast fists had won him fight after fight, and title after title. At the age of 26, he was in his boxing prime and feared by all. Above all, he was stylish.

Yet just before the defence of his world welterweight title against Jimmy Doyle he'd woken up in a terrible sweat.

Later, in his autobiography, Robinson recalled the dream that had so upset him:

DATE:
June 1947

PLACE:
New York, USA

"DOYLE WAS IN THE RING WITH ME. I HIT WITH A FEW GOOD PUNCHES AND HE WAS ON HIS BACK, HIS BLANK EYES STARING UP AT ME, AND I WAS STARING DOWN AT HIM, not knowing what to do, and the referee was moving in to count to ten and Doyle still wasn't moving a muscle. In the crowd I could hear people yelling...

"HE'S DEAD, HE'S DEAD!"

Robinson shared his concern with his trainer George Gainsford and manager Larry Atkins:

"for God's sake, call off this fight. I feel something really bad is going to happen!"

Both men talked with him, telling him that his worries were natural for a boxer. But that didn't mean anything disastrous was going to happen. "Don't be ridiculous," said Atkins, "dreams don't come true. I'd be a millionaire if they did!" **In the end, it took a priest to soothe Robinson and convince him to go ahead with the important fight.**

oyle and Robinson slugged it out for seven rounds. Both men took a lot of punishment, but Doyle was weakening. In the eighth round Robinson saw an opening and dazed Doyle with a DOUBLE RIGHT to the stomach and head. Then a LEFT HOOK to the jaw put Doyle on the canvas. **He fell heavily, cracking the back of his head with a sickening thud**.

Robinson stared down at his motionless opponent, as if he was experiencing his terrible dream again. For a brief moment Doyle's hand fluttered towards the ropes, before the referee declared the fight at an end. Doyle never regained consciousness. The following afternoon he died of head injuries. Sugar Ray was torn by the tragedy, and always haunted by his warning dream.

Uncanny History of Sugar Ray Robinson

Robinson was born as **Walker Smith** in Detroit, Michigan, in 1920. He enjoyed a very successful amateur career, winning all **85** of his contests.

He turned professional in 1940 and was victorious in his first **40** fights. He fought on until finally retiring in 1965, at the age of 44.

Of his **201** professional bouts Robinson won **175**, and he was never knocked out or "stopped" by another boxer.

After **retiring** he turned to acting in movies and on TV. He also did a lot to help young people.

Robinson died of natural causes on 12 April 1989, aged 67 — but to his very last days he was always plagued by his dream 42 years before of...
"THE RING OF DEATH".

Sugar Ray Robinson in dynamic action when he was world middleweight champion in 1951.

Theory 1 ⇨ Mind Messages

New York psychiatrist Montague Ullman was bugged by one question:

When our waking minds are no longer active, is it possible for us to be influenced by suggestions?

34

Many of Ullman's patients referred to dreams that happened to himself — events which the patients could not possibly have known about.

Was Ullman sending messages to his patients without realising it?

Ullman set up a **"dream laboratory"**. While one person was asleep another person, called a "sender", would concentrate on a picture. After the subjects had woken up, they were asked what they could remember. There were misses, but sometimes there was a remarkable similarity between the sender's picture and the subject's memory of the dream...

Had Sugar Ray Robinson received a bad "dream message", warning him of disaster in the ring?

RING OF DEATH

The Russian scientist and doctor Vasili Kasatkin began to examine the connection between his patients' illnesses and their dreams.

One student came to him with a terrifying story: almost every night he dreamed of a **giant python** strangling him. Kasatkin could find nothing wrong with the young man. **Yet, about a year later, he became paralysed.**

In another example, a woman dreamed of being crushed by earth — two months before it was discovered she had a lung disease.

35

Kasatkin concluded that there is a "**DREAM BAND**" in the brain. This alerts the mind to tiny changes in the health of patients.

Perhaps the anxieties that Jimmy Doyle felt about the fight had been picked up by Sugar Ray Robinson's "dream band".

It was certainly an experience he was never to forget.

Last Requests

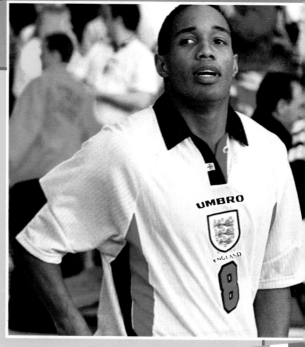

Paul Ince,

the England footballer, does not like putting his shirt on until he has come out of the players' tunnel. Another of his superstitions is to be last out of the tunnel and onto the field — a big problem when he is the team captain! Ince is not strange in this respect: Jack Charlton, England World Cup winner in 1966 and later successful manager of Ireland, was another who insisted on being last out of the dressing-room.

Bright Spark!

The Italian motor-cyclist Carlo Ubbiali, nine times world champion in the 1950s, retired safely after many successful years in this dangerous sport. He claimed that his survival record was down to a SPARK-PLUG that he always carried to bring him luck. Many other top sportsmen believe in their "talismans".

Card players are famous for their superstitions. Many people blow on the cards while shuffling the pack, or get up and walk round their chair or the table three times in a certain direction.

Some players will stop playing bridge, an advanced form of whist, if a **BLACK ACE** falls to the ground during the game.

Black Drop

Empty Promises

The sight of a cross-eyed woman is supposed to be unlucky in baseball — but the sight of a truckload of **EMPTY BARRELS** brings luck!

This strange sign of good fortune was born at the height of popularity of the New York Giants team. A series of victories was believed to happen when such a truck passed the stadium.

So the manager had to pay a driver to bring a similar load past the ballpark on the days they were playing there ...

THE IMPOSSIBLE JOURNEY

Mr Wilmot was returning home on board the sailing ship CITY OF LIMERICK, crossing from Liverpool to New York. For days the sea was rough and the journey was a SICKENING ROLLER-COASTER RIDE. At last the storms eased, and Mr Wilmot climbed into his bunk and closed his eyes. Contentedly, he fell asleep and began a pleasant dream. He saw Mrs Wilmot appear at the door of his cabin, in her nightdress. She stopped, hesitating when she saw that he was sharing with another male passenger. But she picked up her courage and tiptoed across the small room. Then she kissed him and left.

DATE:

1863

PLACE:

SS *City of Limerick*, crossing the Atlantic Ocean

Smiling at such a lovely image.

Mr Wilmot woke up — only to find his cabin-mate leaning over the top bunk and glaring at him.

"How dare you, Sir, allow a woman into our room dressed like that during the hours of darkness. What will the other passengers say?"

Mr Wilmot couldn't think of a sensible reply. He explained that he did not have a girlfriend with him, and that the "woman" was his wife — even though she was several hundred kilometres away at home! He admitted that it didn't sound exactly convincing.

Mr Wilmot arrived home and was even more puzzled to discover that his wife knew about the incident in the cabin. She **had** been there!

She recalled **floating across the dark ocean, landing on the stern of the ship and walking down cold metal steps** — until she found her husband's cabin. Inside, she felt daunted by the stranger staring at her, but she had come too far to turn back. Quickly, she gave her sleeping husband a kiss ... and returned to her bed almost at once.

Theory 1 ⇨ Dreams of a Loving Couple

When people know each other really well, such as close friends or married couples, their thoughts are often very similar. Some researchers believe this could be **telepathy**—communication by thought.

Mr and Mrs Wilmot may have had identical dreams because they were both worried about each other at exactly the same time.

Theory 2 ⇨ An "Out of Body" Experience

There have been reports of people "leaving their bodies", and then seeing themselves and those around them still asleep. Others recall being able to project their body "doubles" across huge distances. There is some evidence that this happens more frequently when people are in that strange space between sleep and consciousness. Mrs Wilmot's exhaustion may have pushed her to the edge of sleep, while concern for her husband freed her "spirit", or a part of herself, to go and look for him.

"Beam me up, Scotty!"

is a favourite phrase of every **Star Trek**® fan. In that series the phenomenon is based on a person "dematerialising" into nothing and then "rematerialising" at the other end;

Theory 3 ⇨ Teleportation

but there are <u>true-life</u> reports of people being able to transport themselves instantly, from one location to another.

It is possible that Mrs Wilmot teleported herself onto the *City of Limerick*.

41

The Israeli magician Uri Geller claims to have psychic powers, including the ability to move objects across huge distances. **Could this "mind over matter"** be increased to transport people?

CATEGORIES OF UNCANNY EXPERIENCES

An opinion poll from 1992 indicated that one in every 30 Americans had undergone some kind of "OBE" or "NDE".

Out of Body Experience (OBE)

An **out of body experience** occurs when a person leaves their body without intending to; it's out of their control. Sometimes witnesses claim to have seen a fine thread, connecting their **"spirit"** to their body.

Near Death Experience (NDE)

A **near death experience** happens when the body is badly hurt, or ill, and may be dying. The **"spirit"** or **"double"** leaves the body, perhaps because of shock. This may be a basic human survival mechanism, allowing the brain or mind to come to terms with an injury before taking over the body again.

British psychologist Dr Susan Blackmore believes that **NDEs are caused by the brain suffering a lack of oxygen, resulting in hallucinations.**

American psychiatrist Dr Elisabeth Kubler-Ross thinks that **NDEs may be the first stage of death** — and possibly the beginning of the journey to the afterlife. She suggests that death can be a peaceful and even joyful experience for many people.

ASTRAL PROJECTION

43

This is the **rarest kind of "OBE"**.
It takes great skill and occurs when
someone leaves their body by choice.
They take their spirit on a journey.

Astral Projection

For thousands of years, deeply religious people have used different styles of
meditation to unlock their souls from the physical prison of their bodies—

and fly to other places. . .

In April 1916, during World War I, a young medical officer waited for take-off. A member of the British Royal Flying Corps, he was being flown to see an urgent case at another airfield.

The plane had not gained enough speed when the pilot tried a sharp turn and it plunged back to the ground in a crash-landing. **The medic was thrown clear and lay as if dead on the ground.** He later recalled:

"Suddenly I was looking down on my body from some 200 feet above it."

He watched as the unhurt pilot and other officers rushed to his side. "My spirit, or whatever you want to call it, was wondering why they were bothering. . .and I remember wishing they would leave it alone."

Soaring above the field, he watched an almost comic rescue team start

out from the hangars. ❯ The ambulance stalled and the

driver leapt out to crank the engine with the starting handle.

❯❯ They had barely set off again when the medical

orderly jumped out and ran back, as if to collect

something he had forgotten. ❯❯❯

Third time lucky, the ambulance

raced towards his body.

Then, with a sharp jerk, his

viewpoint changed. He could feel a

stimulant being poured down his throat — and he

opened his eyes to the normal world again. In hospital, his

commanding officer listened to his story and checked out the

details. He was amazed to find they were all correct. Yet the

injured doctor could not have seen what the rescue team was

doing — because the hangars were completely hidden

from the airfield by a steep hill.

Really Useful Words and Phrases

 TO KILL A KING

bailiff powerful law officer of the King; an early form of policeman

consumed eaten up

coven a gathering of witches

Devil's mark skin blemish of any kind thought to be caused by the Devil in witches

fanciful made-up, unbelievable

marrow soft tissue in the hollow parts of bones

midwife woman who helps deliver babies at birth

noble high-ranking landowner; early form of aristocrat

oath solemn and binding pledge, especially to a god

ordained ordered to happen

persecution hounding and hurting people because of their beliefs

Satan most common name given to the Devil

sceptical doubting, not taking at "face value"

sieve meshed kitchen utensil for sifting flour

sorcerer person who casts spells with the help of spirits

supernatural greater than normal, breaking the "laws of nature"

warlock male witch or sorcerer

 THE MAD MONK

aristocracy titled members of the wealthy classes

cancer life-threatening disease that destroys the body's cells

Communist political party believing in the sharing of all work and property

conspiracy secret plot

courtier important person at the court of the Tsar

Eastern Orthodox Church eastern branch of Christianity that broke off from the Church of Rome

haemophilia medical condition leading to excessive bleeding when any blood vessel is hurt or cut

hypnotic able to command total attention

inherited passed down by previous generations, usually parents

peasants rural working classes, usually landless

pilgrimage journey to holy places by devout believers (pilgrims)

scapegoat person who takes the blame, even though they may be innocent

superstitious ignorant and illogical belief in the supernatural

Tsar ruler (Emperor) of Russia

Tsarina Empress of Russia

 HECTOR THE HOMING DOG

First Officer next man in charge of a ship after the Captain

instincts natural impulses in animals (that is, not learned)

investigate look into

landmark natural or artificial object or building that stands out from the landscape

magnetism natural force of attraction closely linked to electricity

organism any living animal or plant

predicting stating what will happen in the future

schedule plan with dates, timetable

46

stowaway person who secretly "stows away" by hiding on a ship or aircraft to be carried free

supernatural greater than normal, breaking the "laws of nature"

telepathic linked minds or communication by thought

vessel any boat or ship

warblers small singing birds

THE RING OF DEATH

amateur person who plays sports without being paid

autobiography book you write about your own life or experience; a biography is a book written about someone else's life

consciousness the state of being aware

"inside the distance" boxing term for winning a contest before its scheduled number of rounds is completed

middleweight boxer who weighs between 67 and 73 kilograms

natural causes death from age as opposed to a specific illness

paralysed inability to use all or parts of the body

professional person who gets paid for playing sports

psychiatrist person who treats illnesses of the mind

round in boxing, the fighting part of the event (lasting three minutes)

"stopped" in boxing, prevented by the referee or helpers from continuing the fight; in the USA it is called a "technical knockout"

superstitious ignorant and illogical belief in the supernatural

talisman object, often inscribed or carved, believed to protect the owner or wearer from evil influences

tragedy extremely sad event

welterweight boxer who weighs between 61 and 67 kilograms

THE IMPOSSIBLE JOURNEY

astral belonging to the stars

consciousness the state of being aware

convincing believable

daunted put off

hangar large shed for planes

hesitate wait because of uncertainty or indecision

indicated showed

matter substances out of which anything is made

medic member of military medical services

meditation relaxing the mind deeply, especially in a spiritual sense; thinking deeply on spiritual matters

opinion poll a survey of people's views on a certain subject

orderly in the forces, a junior rank detailed to carry out orders for a more senior person

phenomenon remarkable thing or event

psychic beyond the physical

psychologist person who studies the human mind and behaviour

stimulant medicine to revive an unconscious person

viewpoint place from which you see things

Index